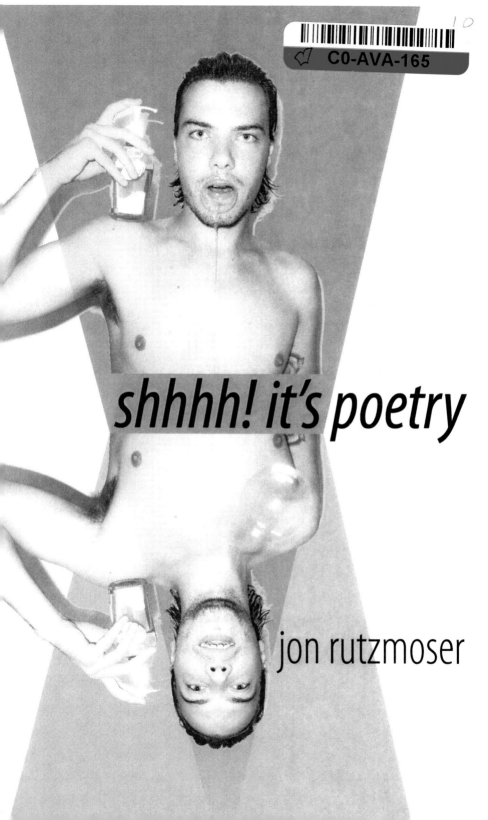

shhhh! it's poetry

jon rutzmoser

shhhh! it's poetry

jon rutzmoser

INSERT

PRESS

Blanc Press Los Angeles
Freedom of the press is limited to those who own one.
When the rim is bent it will press against the works and
impede the proper action of the currents.

SHHHH! IT'S POETRY
by Jon Rutzmoser © 2014
Insert Blanc Press, 2014
ISBN: 978-0-9911092-0-3

Acknowledgments
Pieces from this collection have previously appeared in *Drunken Boat* and *Joyland*.

Many thanks to my family and friends for their unwavering love and support. Thanks also to the following people for reading earlier versions of this manuscript: Kate Coltun, Hilary Darling, Travis Diehl, Nicholas Katzban, Jon Lindsey, Anthony McCann, Maggie Nelson, Ani Raya-Flores, Mady Schutzman, and Brad Strong. Special thanks to Jon Wagner for his unbelievably gracious guidance and to Kirsty Singer and Jennifer Styperk for caring deeply for this project through its various manifestations. Many thanks also to Mathew Timmons for the invaluable edits and to Insert Blanc Press for making my book. Lastly, eternal thanks to Amanda Montei for showing me joy.

for my mom susan
and my pop kurt

it does
exist!

part one / complexicon

after ph_ll_s

i.

somewhere in a winter garden in winter
garden florida between a memory
and a low resolution video feed
i picture myself as you are
upside down dangling
a young girl's hair
sweeping the
rug under a
mother's
bed

ii.

milk
spilling
on an empty
box of chocolates
she blames the bunny
remembering or raising her
voice the name susan
a flick of the ear
a compulsion
to hurt the
one she
loves

iii.

susan... hiding... objects...
in a hole... fingering...polaroids...
in a box... marked... susan...
coming... across... her...
faceless... torso... and thighs...
naked... you are...already...
speaking... in fine... particles...
out there... surfacing... the object...
its fill flash... makes up... thickens it...
phyllis... scored... well...
above her... hairless... c-word...

iv.

now here... near the bed...

your jaw clicking... mechanically...
in a thunderstorm... and...

you're asking... again and...
again... "who's phyllis?" and...

"mom
who
is
phyllis?"

her face turning... its redness...
pausing... and pausing
nowhere... near here...

death is alone... earless and sad...
singing a vincent gallo lullaby...

phyllis... your pet bunny...
and... phyllis... your mother...

you were adopted... susan...

                              coughing...
                              swallowing...
                              soapy water...

v.

alone in your room… you are watching yourself…
you are watching yourself… naked on screen…

filming yourself… hoisting your hips…
hold it right there… as you hoist your own hips…

your ass in your palms… your own sweaty palms…
your hands and your palms… your elbows and palms…

they're cymbals on springs… ringing on springs…
clashing on springs… your elbows on springs…

your shoulders and toes… they're curling on springs…
you're tucking your chin… and singing her name…

phillis… on the precipice… raised to the wind…

the lens… spinning and aligning… all by itself…
the *is*… in *phillis*… your wet baby blues…

take me now… wow me… to your stupid place…
susan… feeling blurred… and important…

our hands… on the bus… with the cord…
the two of us… on the bus… with the cord…

we pull it… and get off… together…
the camera… it films itself… capsizing…

vi.

chocking your half-assed identity…
hacking her name in alpha-bits…

wandering through the market…
licking pop labels and nipples…
are you my mother fucker…
screaming apples to apples…

while biting your tongue…
i'm just playing with it…

playing hopscotch…
with a butterscotch…

playing squash…
with a butternut…

your perfect hands…
for making notes…

for tapping secrets…
whispering secrets…

and smoothing skin…
a giant clitoris…

susan… who is…
phillis… now…

hanging on…
by a thread…

vii.

but… you are real… susan…
you are real… and… you share…
a name… with my mother…

wanting you… to want to…
eat children's cereal… and watch…
saturday morning cartoons…

darling… spoon me… this second…
this hand couch holds…it may not last…
much longer… than… commercial breaks…

wanting you… to want to…
call… that number… susan…
i am… in love… with her…

viii.

phyllis with a y... my biological mom...

i was adopted... when i was sixteen...
i contacted her... she didn't want to meet...

gave me the whole... it would be too hard...
gave me the whole... shit would be too hard...

so when i turned eighteen... i said fuck it...
and got it... it's helvetica neue you know...

taking a polaroid... writing in sharpie...
on the frame... watching it process...

sending it to her... along with a copy...
of my mother... her naked photo...

(two peas on an ipod shuffle)

requiring... and getting confirmation...
picking up your touch screen phone...
sliding... and typing... and having...
to text the message... to somehow...
exist... in multiple places buzzing...

appropriate measures

i.

exhibit a: y? bc i am not u…

and mouthing "elephant juice"
back and forth in each other's ears
two young artists meet masturbating
in a closet at a costume party

                                        ready or not—

they convince the others, by
throwing tomatoes, that they
were just catching up
were just becoming cinema

                                        they say—

susan and rutzy sitting in a tree
k=i=s=s=i=n=g
first comes love then comes marriage
then comes little jonny in the mother fucking void

coming in umbros and shin guards
he makes eyes in the dark with
a young girl—
nay, a soccer mom

that
fateless
idiot asking
through the door
are we the beckhams?

later that night we make a full length
fuck tape culminating in a scene
where i gouge out my eyes
with an eight inch cock

and the buzzing clit
hook spits fake
blood on a
mirror

we title it
together

> *exhibit be:*
> *soccercles' oedipus rex*

ii.

but here's jonny with his coke bottle
glasses dripping with juice and panting

"i'll make an art book out of you"
and they will simply never align—

> my body of work and
> my body of work

splash / susan

i created you twice now... say it...
say thank you... like you mean it...

saying her first word...
at sea world...

put your hands together...
the ball pit is empty...

it's filling....... with water...

the flash and
the tile and
the skin

the shining / gradient / moisture

thirty-three splintered hands...
scrubbing the redness...
off a white fence...

"stick 'um up cock tucker"

turning a real gun on…
your fuck-you finger…
she blows smoke rings…
spreading her ass cheeks…
on stage… revealing mystic truths…

(lips sinking
in the dark)

                    "you kiss
                    your mother
                    with that
                    blowhole?"
"you don't
even know
the words"

iii.

photographic backdrops for shaved pubic hair…

only a carrot in a goddamn carrot hole…

iv.

exhibit see: the world no longer exists...
susan... eat your breakfast for dinner...

a toy gun under my pillow...
we've all got options...

a stained *got milk?* ad...
we've all got a voice-over...

chewing on ice he loses a tooth...
later she finds it under the bed...
a sort of greenness true to form...
drifts in through the window...

the dog... now clean...
drags his ass on the carpet...

the film will yellow... over time...
you know... the bird's beak...

its pornographic clicking...
it's just wormlessness...

the film... time...
the bird's beak...

 it's pornographic clicking...

v.

the sky is alive…
her ass up in the air…

as the crow flies…
as the kitten laps…

i am not your inkblot maid…
cries a mother in leather…

but you are…
you are here…

(waking the baby)

and up up goes the bird…
towards the gutters and static…

her hands clasping the buzz…
folding foil on hangers…

how does one even fuck a television?

vi.

learning to tie a windsor…
her odd eyes crossed…

the imprint on her head…
it is a wormhole…

just tickle the blueness…
a fowl flying in circles…

he loves commercials…
says it to hear it be said…

then he says it again
crossing his fingers…

a smile in hand is worth…
everyone singing together…

two birds in the bush…
no birds in no bush…

vii.

and how can that cow have both udders and bull horns…
and how can we know when language goes missing…

and how can a kitten say no with her whiskers…
and how can a baby speak before flying…

and how can a dog tell the difference…
and how can a hen be so frank…

and how can a car wreck…
and how can a crane…

not not mean…
mother…

viii.

the
quest
ion marks...

exhibit de:
ontological
ethics

a slash / is a slash / is a slash?

baby / in / the / air

shhhh!

it's
around
the corner

c / o / m / p / l / e / x / i / c / o / n

open letters

how words work / how we are just

three / no. / more / no.
there / no. / more / no.
more / no. / there / no.

there / i said it
shit's / contagious
shit's / contiguous
there / no there

a total / eclipse / of the heart

finding it / as in / experience

        but mother fuck
        your metaphors
        it's you i love
        goddamn it

like an apology
like a goddamn
appalling e note
for not swearing

     feeding me footnotes
     for breakfast and
     wiping my
     asshole

  your digits
  swirling
  deep
  like

the grammar of a disco ball

spinning in circles
throwing darts at a map
on the side of a barn door

exhibit e: ieio
exhibit f: you seek a _____
exhibit gee: ode

"god
exits   (sigh)
                    i jest
                    no wit"

exhibit h: hanging up
exhibit h: his history
exhibit h: is susan

exhibit eye: see you pee (up)

pop / goes / the / easel

he a young boy dressed as an artist requests that other artists piss on him
he a young artist marked by an artist addresses the problem of origins
he flips a coin one thousand times and stands on his head

she a young girl dressed as an artist requests a glass of mott's from him
she a young artist marked by the artist addresses his broken language
she flips the camera the bird and pisses on his arm

two / young / artists / address / shit / together

ms. _____
3343 daniels road
winter garden, fl 34787

a postcard invitation to a performance
on one side in helvetica neue
as *feminine subject*

and on the other side
in helvetica neue
piss on me

please

exhibit j: jouissance
exhibit j: *ontos* on
exhibit j: jonr fucker
exhibit k: kick (one or be)
exhibit l: ewd
exhibit m: others (obviously)
exhibit n: ew / d
exhibit o: a screaming emoticon
exhibit p: i=s=s=i=n=g
exhibit q: you art
exhibit are: rose

you are
making a list
of people to invite

on the one hand believing
that they will attend and on the
other hand knowing that they won't

1. abramović, marina	14. irigaray, luce	27. piper, adrian
2. bee, susan	15. jackson, shelley	28. place, vanessa
3. benglis, lynda	16. kelly, mary	29. perloff, marjorie
4. bergvall, caroline	17. kristeva, julia	30. schneemann, carolee
5. butler, judith	18. kruger, barbara	31. sherman, cindy
6. calle, sophie	19. levine, sherrie	32. spahr, juliana
7. chicago, judy	20. madonna	33. spivak, gayatri
8. emin, tracey	21. mavor, anne	34. sturtevant, elaine
9. gaga, lady	22. mayer, bernadette	35. wearing, gillian
10. grey, sasha	23. minnis, chelsey	36. kraus, chris
11. haraway, donna	24. mullen, harryette	37. krauss, rosalind
12. hilton, paris	25. myles, eileen	38. waldrop, rosmarie
13. holzer, jenny	26. ono, yoko	39. walker, kara

(to be placed on
the list please text
exhibit s: u sans
to 215.407.6753

to be without / a slight / projection
finishing off / a stroke / a letter / a text
piddling / the space / you're in / it flows

dear _____,
   "after you"

"you are a dancer" but mother may i
have the question of how to explain anything
to anyone anymore in wendy's with laptops we save
as as if it's the best left handed three fingered function we've
got to rename without losing anything unless we lose everything
transcribing it onto a napkin and folding itself over twice and eating it
you throwing tiny nuggets of chicken at my face while i play the knife game
"that plastic won't cut shit!" and at all costs doing my best not to gag
remembering trying ketchup for the first time and gagging inside
a wendy's much like this you telling me to try it again saying
"taste buds take time to adjust" i did and it was better
or rather i knew what to expect swallowing swords
and shitting out words repetition as side line
stepping the knowing as if knowing and
i know you are older and slower now
and i just want to thank you now

the pointed bra in all
of its incarnations
tells the half
truth and
spits

dear _____,
"after you"

mother /   may i?

mother /   may i ask you a question?
may i ask you a strange question?
may i borrow your panties?
may i wear your panties?

mother /   will you photograph me wearing your panties?
will you call him and ask permission?

mother /   may i please explain?
may i show you how to use the camera?
may i call you susan?
may i ask you to smile?

mother /   will you call me susan? and
will you ask me to smile?

dear _____,

"after you"

they call it a swirlie. you say swooshie. either way my face is in the
shitter and you are flushing and you are filming. documentation we
think is important. we piss in the shower our heads dripping and
straining. and all i can think is your toenails are perfect. and all you
can think is my nipples are perfect. two lovers perfecting the art of the
phone call. and i miss you but you are here. and i am blending you not
because you are the same people and not because i don't value your
difference but precisely because i am sitting on my new toilet with my
new pants on. and you are writing or sleeping or thinking about our last
meal or our next meal and i am feeling like i understand better now.
and i want you to know that it is because of you and the wedding and
the blowjob and the keys are sounding like vibrations about to reach
my fingers. and my hair is still crooning. feet sticking to the tile. i want
this forever. and i hope everyone can someday experience what we
have. not feel bad and smile in pictures. smoking and eating tacos and
revisiting such happy thoughts while deificating.

dear _____,
"after you"

and...shhhh!

it's just poetry
it's not just poetry

it's just poetry
it's not just poetry

it's not not important
you asshole

you lovely
exhibitionist

he sits in the fountain
photocopying his ass

we throw coins
killing two birds

it was an earthy hue
the sky was old

interlewd

seven + ways to score a penis

i.
tuck your penis / the pen is mightier / phone your mother
read a book to her / write some poems / write some poems for her

(repeat)

ii.
fuck your penis / the pen is smuttier / own your mother
eat a book of hers / right some wrongs / right some wrongs for her

(repeat)

iii.
pluck your penis / the pen is metaphor / clone your mother
knead a mold of her / cite some songs / cite some songs for her

(repeat)

iv.
buck your penis / the pen is typical / throne your mother
bleed and cook for her / bite your tongue / bite your tongue for her

(repeat)

v.
shuck your penis / the pen is retractable / moan your mother
ease words in her ear / husk her name / husk her name for her

(repeat)

vi.
suck your penis / the pen is mouthable / displace your mother
spread your seed for her / gnaw a bone / gnaw a bone for her

(repeat)

vii.
chuck your penis / the pen is throwable / trace your mother
shed a tear for her / shoot some skeet / shoot some skeet for her

(repeat)

when / reflecting / being

begin / with / the meat

                 as in...
        you peel potatoes
        you say potato
        you don't say
        bringing all the
        boys to the yard

        you read descartes
        you say descartes
        you don't say
        making the bed
        the tools in the yard

in slow motion
the mullet breathes
through the milkshake

did you see that?
gargling pop rocks
and not dying twice

sign / sigh / sing

good night sheep
counting backwards
from now on

my pants are off
and i'm trying to
figure things out

foggy like the other
morning fingering
your panties
next to my
drawer
the ones
forgotten
on purpose
smelling them
pretending to get
excited the toothless
guy at the laundromat huffing
deep blue velvet silk on my septum
it feels like a choir stepping on fingernails

revolutionary susan

pants who needs them?

who needs them is said
fuck you underwear boy
panting walking with a lack

overhead a superhero flies
backwards humming and
pissing herself with the fair
songs of what's-his-face

my name's no longer susan
spit fucking ourselves under
humvees and dancing on
concrete hand prints

it's not fair to be punished
for your friend's rigid nipples
"those bowed legs are awful"
said the leg man to no one

i am sorry but when i said
her new tits looked good
i was referring to her hair
the incisions in her armpits

phillis reads an artnews
taking her morning shit
crooning in a kazoo
talking on the phone

he loves me not
he loves me

"hey this is jon
leave me a message
and i'll call you back
mother beep"

"hey baby it's me
we are just products
and for today only
all sales are final"

butterfly kisses
as a dingleberry
drops slowly

in our city naked / current artforum

your culture / fucks well with global lust
it is a brazilian wax on main st
on page 58 / *gravity index*

and photographs of pink dildos flap on ends of a seesaw
yellow in it's post post-apocalyptic essence
it's nov. '74 all over again!
it's crooked smiles
over teetering toes

it's in the air and we can taste it sweetheart

the fish gets tossed from gloved hand to gloved hand
the working rubber smears and rubs skin and scales
and wet concrete the wind and folds and sacks
through patches of course hair interested flesh

it condenses uphill

inside track lights glisten
prophylactics numb the
would be brilliant pink
the licentious utilitarian
it's political and
it's just asking for it!
homogenous floor tape
the difference between
fondu and fondue
we wax intellectual
the security guards
always yelling at us
to put our phones
back in our pockets

and outside our bicycles
locked up upside down
screaming to be fucked
in the sun or sculpture garden
the neighborhood teens
if they did exist
would gather around and crank the
pedals to make ice cream
their green shadows

the post-end returning

failure is part of this game and i hate you for letting me win
failure is part of this game and i hate you for letting me win

failure is part of this game and i hate you for letting me win
failure is part of this game and i hate you for letting me win

failure is part of this game and i love you for letting me win
failure is part of this game and i love you for letting me   in

failure is my middle name and i thank you for giving me   it
failure is my middle name and i love you for giving me shit

failure is my middle name and i hope you will give me your piss
failure is my middle name and i hope you won't mind if i quit

failure might muddle my mouth might muddle my mouth a bit
failure might cuddle the couch might huddle the coach and spit

failure might set out to win and get put on the injured list
failure might drool on a hand and rub it all over my tit

milk me you sweet little failed bitch of an other

i want you to want to want to

inside a white cube there is a white cube
there is a heaping mound of polaroids
a black-framed artist in underwear
is fisting a pickle jar and yelling
in a can with a string and
sucking on conflict free
fingers to be seen
and i dream i
am fucking
you
in
moma's
bathroom
stuffing the
difference in the
seems of the mirror
tasting the brown under
the red acrylic and all around
teeth chatter on bulging black leather
a voice from buried speakers mutters the title
                              over and over again—

                         i want you to want to want to
                         i want you to want two. want two
                         i want you too. one two one two
                         i want you to want two on two
                         i want you to want to un-chew

          (wanting to undo
                  to command z himself)

eye / one hue / to one hue / to one hue
i won't use two / won't use two / why won't you?
i / one / you / two /

a video of two lovers wrestling in mud puddles
carrot shavings sway in the projected light
someone or something on the other end of the string

"fucking fuck me?
you mother fucker!
did you just fucking call
yourself an artist?

and the questions matter

after the money shot

he lines the city block with fuck dolls
a bank explodes the paint and bags
the slow expanding crack in the ceiling

get the masking tape and bake me a cake
"it's all about the walter benjamins baby"
a young poet or artist as fast as you can

glueing hair on a statue "i am a statue"
says the statue my stash is for sale
pushing the rubber cock into the pocket

pussy flossing with fishnets the dog laps
a latte he tapes a feather to his finger
toothless he tickles the child in a bart

simpson mask his mother hisses something
about the death of the author *exhibit t: it*
for the time being, begins here

wiping it makes magic
the envoy's no longer
i believe in joy now

and
i believe
now enjoy

to the world
the naked snow
angle only pretends

to be dead the carolers
knock on the 26th day of july
i find you fat and green in a dumpster

but the cat came back / the very next day
the cat came back / they thought he was a goner
but the cat came back / he just wouldn't stay away

dear _____,

postmodern love
don't even get me started
let's get retarded in here

your metaphors are so salty like
i dream i am fucking you
in the moma bathroom

like me fucking you
like being you
in the moma bathroom

wondering how many posts
would suffice in prefacing modernity
would you be like enough?

context is a funny think you know

danto jocks philo box project
project thought onto art object
object to discerning from import
import meaning for the word it

replace word object with subject
subject the reader to construct
construct our very own present
present meaning for the word it

language must warrant this contract
contract the current hot content
content me with your best conduct
conduct meaning for the word it

confuse the meaning as abstract
abstract the terms of our discourse
discourse the texture as extract
extract meaning for the word it

what is in a question anymore?
compression? re-save the jpg
four or more times and view
at one hundred percent

record yourself singing
the trashmen
diving in dumpsters
surfing the web to
find yourself monthly

mega pixel brillo box
master pistel lip botox
misty plexel dumb like fox
maxi pickle dildo face

part two / post!modern

do not let me be a nazi schatzi!

i.

20 february 1939
you attend the rally at the garden
you are arrested, convinced
language is
           the silent card
           stops the clock
and i love you
for what he
has become

ii.

a man… [with] a plan
a canal… [in] panama

it's not… [not] a palindrome
the room and its blueness
it's green like the blueness
the gray then there's blueness

"did extermination camps have grass?"
the doctored greenness tickles the fence posts

"it's within us all… just pick a card, son."

in a rocking chair… he digs a hole
he throws the game… "just go to sleep"
he knows it's wrong… he cannot sleep
he mutters words… through cookie crumbs
his coffee breath… it browns his face
he ties the string… it blues his face

the cream smell stink…
the doorway chip…
the blackened spit…

it stains the wood

iii.

they say it was his favorite
that naughty matryoshka

the one designed to look
like an inflatable fuck doll

how she would nest herself
just sort of disappear

iv.

it's not a question of causality…
it does not even have a question…
language is… [just] language…

a young boy sings… to god… and or his father…
                          and or his father's father… for all to hear…
a young boy singing… to god… and or his father…
                          and or his father's father… for all to hear…

my father's father was a nazi…
my father's father was a baker…
my father's father was in the bund…

                    (for all to hear)

                    to bake bread
                    to sell bread
                    to play soccer

v.

germantown / philadelphia / 1933

15,000 ghosts attend
the 250th   anniversary
the 1st   settlement

the   united singers
                   singing to   each   other
                   singing to   their   dead   ears
the   language   falling
to   the   folded   napkins
of   fugitive   gods

he   went   to   be
                   to   berlin
                   to   the   olympics

his   "image"   moving
saluting

                   an / erect / arm

and i cannot believe that he
believed in anything at all
but my father believes
and with his father
his armband he
says it aloud
he says he
will never
show
me

to   ignore the   sound   of   tears   he
pokes   the   page   with a   pen pretending
to   play   the knife   game   with a   bic

singing / language / tactile / sharp / hairy

vi.

                                    and,
jonny you mustn't feed the pigeons
the doves are different than pigeons
the bread is not for the pigeons
the rainbow is water and light

we hug
            in the cold
            in our jackets
            in the "showers"

                        and i swear i cry like god
                            sing the saddest most
                        melancholic fucking song

                                        .

vii.

in the seventh grade i go to a new school
a public school in a proud jewish community

and only because it first appears
on a pinstriped soccer jersey
does our name ever exist
on an invitation to attend and
responding that i will attend
i learn to say "mozel tov!"

but that year in july
he dies on your birthday

"he shit himself
on his death bed"

you call me schatzi… tell me my bad blood is no longer…
and on 9 november exactly 20 years after the wall fell…
ears and bells and phones all ring simultaneously…

viii.

shhhh!

it's over
it's over now

tri(x)ter

eating trix for three days straight
       writing   (letters)

the trickster in the narrative
it is the narrative itself

the limp rabbit says something
puts on his spectacles

imagine 1,000 others in a field
at the same time, you can't

let them bounce about for one hour
let them melt into the flowers

                        "silly faggot
                        dicks are
                        for chicks!"

(and the mob circles
and spits laughter
into a hole)

because why is the wrong answer
because words say so
and you say so

"the end is near!" or
"the end is here!"
it is no longer

my mouth / my bowl / my bowels

                  we all want to say it

shhhh! it's around the corner bunny whoop there it is
shhhh! it's around the corner bunny whoop there it is
shhhh! it's around the corner bunny whoop there it is

bunny bunny bunny bunny whoop bunny whoop bunny bunny bunny bunny
bunny bunny bunny bunny whoop bunny whoop bunny bunny bunny bunny
bunny bunny bunny bunny whoop bunny whoop bunny bunny bunny bunny

dear _____,
       (i'm here to recruit you)

eeny / meeny / miny / moe
catcha / baby / by its / toe

if he / hollers / let him / go
eeny / meeny / miny / moe

my / mother / told / me / to
pick / the / very / best / one

and / that / is / y / o / u

eat // repeat // and // and // and eating // and / and // eating
and repeating and // and repeating / eating // and / and
repeating eating // and repeating // and and // eating
and eating and and // and repeating // and and // repeating

and / and / and / and

        shit

           sever

       lasting
               and a line is always already scored
               and the score always already exists
               as the thing we always already do
it is only this // and not the end // that is
alone / in the shadow / or / debris / of / monoliths

                       exhibit t: it
                   milk me sugar
                     i don't know
                   milk me sugar
                    help me grow
                   milk me sugar
                  soft and sweet
                     til the cows
                   come home
                 mother fucker

shhhh!
what's the matter with you /
you say / it's nothing /
for god's sake /

dear ,

nouns or no nouns? pronouns or no pronouns? nouns are pro pro-
nouns. pronouns are pro nouns and pro pronouns. but what happens
if a noun goes no on pronouns? or worse yet, no on other nouns. and
pronouns show no woe for fellow pronouns? or nouns? a professional
noun is called a pro noun. a professional pronoun, a pro pronoun. pro-
fessional clowns run around and around. professional clowns are pro
clowns. clowns or no clowns? pro clowns or no pro clowns?

      q: is it possible to juggle with cereal?
      a: don't talk with your mouth full.

nouns and clowns. nouns are clowns. pronouns and pro clowns? bozo
and pronouns and faux clowns and krusty. as a project. project nouns
and pronouns. a project projecting nouns and pronouns. a project
projecting nouns and pronouns using nouns and pronouns onto nouns
and pronouns and clowns and pro clowns and faux clowns and so on
and so on and so on we go. bounding across previously bound bound-
aries. we found ourselves bound together as boundary bounders. our
clowning unbound the boundaries. as noun and pronoun bounders.
bound together in cities and towns, that is pronouns in nouns and
other nouns. bound together for both success and failure.

dear ,

the refrigerator buzzes loudly and this has everything to do with everything. metonymy. in order to fully understand it i will eventually have to trade underwear with as many tonys as possible. to place their name between me and my work would. to place me / tony / my work back on the page. the tiny balls are slowly filtering milk through pores and an even smaller bubble forms at the base of the spoon. i eat it. i imagine that the blue and the green balls all unite into tiny earth-like trix globes and deep deep deep down on the rocky topography of one of those land portions, inside my bowl, we both sit and discuss the significance. typography is impotent. i pour you a bowl. ryan trecartian. and i pour me another. and we look at each other and smile and pick up our spoons and take beautiful bites. never breaking eye contact and never stopping to notice the milk dripping down our chins. or why rainbows happen. i promise agnosticism, but sometimes i talk to your god—a kid flipping coins or pulling rose petals to see if he cares. shitting my pants, i write a poem. three tired little balls smear my cheeks. sugar deposits along my gums. the milk trickles down my throat and everything is clean. my spit and tongue i swallow. sticky film remains.

dear ,

he a young man dressed as a boy dressed as a rabbit pours a bowl of trix before you a young woman dressed as a boy dressed as a rabbit pouring a bowl of trix before school. where you and school are both things and lack the capability, that is to say, it is arbitrary. to mean anything which is not beyond a thing's borders. reader. borders. flannel buttons. tender mutton chops. suspenders. suspension bridges. brooklyn. whitman. remembering. khaki pleats. bambi and thumper feet excited first feature seen. thunder meets buzz lightyear years later. crash. flash. the flash. the lighting doubles you. the screen doubles you. you and i stay in the w. george w. xyz. zip it. misuse. "excuse me miss. you seem to have forgotten yourself." it's cartoonish to think people think this way. what's up doc hollywood means more to me today and that's all folks and michael j. fox and julie warner and warner brothers. and the 20th century space jam and michael jordan bugs me and you're twenty three and your eyes are yellow and the gap between us as if mellow yellow vs. mountain dew is relevant and even in a white studio when lit right shadows highlight objects. color accents. drive an accent. shape shapes. circle around the block. box out. box office. ali. foreman grill. nelly's grill. brillo box.

oh dear! _____,

like an irrational fear
born the year she died
born the day she
dropped flowers
in an empty box
on the corner

the fork on the street
the fiddle
they exhibit you
exhibit u: yourself
your five little fingers
exhibit v :o i.d. yrself
yr five little selves
they double you
exhibit w: omen

and an elderly
lady just
burns

and

i am not
not talking
desire here she
literally is burning
from a cigarette next
to her sleeping face and
her shopping cart and blanket
ablaze with emotion i try to wake
her by shaking her bones in the heat
but she still sleeps softly through her nose
as if she were the girl with the face and the bag

the world in headlights

filling a ziplock with trix
i slide it and lock it green
my apartment is too hot
i can't write in my underwear
i walk to starbucks
a bell rings
i order water
there's a girl
sitting in the corner
i know her face
i'm almost certain
she knows mine
but she never looks up
i walk by her to go to the bathroom
i walk by her to go back from the bathroom
she never looks up
a stranger steps on my foot
the hurt reminds me of the dead blow thumb smash yabba dabba do!
i limp back to my table
begin popping the little bagged balls
bubble wrap
successfully rupturing
the trix into fruity pebbles
tiny balls to even tinier flakes
general mills to post
contemporary to prehistoric
froot loops aren't safe
being other-than-itself
now concerning kix and
apple jacks and
everything is
continuing to work
the now fruity pebbles
into grains of sand
telling myself this
is how god feels
picturing fred flintstone's man feet
moving his prehistoric car
i walk towards the girl with the face
and hand her the bag

post!modern

and a women at the gas station is screaming insisting that her thirteen and a half gallons are not there
and the attendant behind the counter sells me cigarettes swearing to god that he could not care less
and please stay behind the yellow line is translated as a row of school girls swing their held hands

and having not grown up in the 40s or 50s he regretfully informs me that something is missing
and she trains herself to function on one meal a day so she can afford to eat in hollywood
and the word fear in white on a black box is left on a moving subway in december

and you apologize for having come too early then realize the condom is broken
and life is shitty i say after realizing that i had taken advantage of your youth
and i mail you a postcard asking you to draw a thousand bunnies for me

and it is snowing and i am definitely not scared of lying down in the dark
and a sign on a locked door asks me to please see attendant for key
and we argue over the difference between fake cocks and dildos

and you say the whole world is racist and misogynistic but you
and somehow this makes us feel like we're gods in a theatre
and you get her initials tattooed in red on your sternum

and then she legally changes her name to whatever
and i can almost taste the goddamn difference
and a glass is never half anything

and i sprint to find the bathroom
and people stop breathing

post!modern

and i dream i am in a library basement archiving years of feminism and sleeping my head on your shoulder
and a child brushes his teeth reciting his favorite knock knock joke again and again in front of a mirror
and the new couple walking in the park looks at the dog squatting and smiles and kisses tenderly
and he recalls the way he felt when he awoke to a perfectly circular blood stain on his pillow
and reading with a semi his hands moving to the sound of a neighbor coughing outside
and his mentor requests that he learn the difference between trauma and word play
and playing guitar for the first time in years his fingers are sore then fall inside her
and inserting a blue highlighter into her vagina she drags it across the page
and 10:48 pm on sat. april 10th marks their first audible farts together
and being allergic to milk he struggles with feeling less than human
and singing together in ecstasy they both slip on banana peels
and he never tells anyone that he fucked the sleeping bag
and he contemplates shaving his ass before the exam
and because you read to me i believe in metaphors
and then she slides off his cold swimming trunks
and he remembers that jesus christ died today
and then they laugh and laugh in the shower
and her ass in those tights from that store
and he remembers it but forgets why
and kissing the inside of her thighs
and he signs his testicle *john kruk*
and vacuum lines in the dark
and the irony itches his ass
and plucking a single hair
and she is bleeding
and he howls out
and they come
and come

exhibit x:
oh boy!

i shit my pants for fun today
          after (you called me) andy

and i say that
i would rather watch
somebody buy their
underwear than read
a book they wrote

and that's what
he said walking
to american apparel
smoking and devising
a plan of economy

it's just poetry so
look at the camera
and ask the sales lady
all flannelled and nippled
to pick a number

to share a glass-bottled coke
her lipstick—

                on   the straw
                on   the camel light
                that broke the back of
                the dove chocolate
                the bunny stain

it is disneyesque... her tasty smile in
the seventh minute of november rain

we sprint home with stolen sharpies...

you write my name in my underwear / i write your name in your underwear
you write my name in your underwear / i write your name in my underwear
you write your name in my underwear / i write my name in your underwear
you write your name in your underwear / i write my name in my underwear

we auction
our bodies
on artnet

(retaining our values)

exhibit y: our underwear

a young motherfucker

a young motherfucker / dressed as a model / films himself
he films himself / undressing / pressing play
we're rolling / he says

he's rolling / on a condom / playing dress up
filming himself / watching the film / blowup
he is watching / blowup / in fast forward

and filming himself / rolling forwards / almost blowing himself
but he cannot / blow himself / his body won't roll enough
the film keeps rolling / and the motherfucker / rolls with it

seeing two lovers… in a field…
the artist desires… the model's desire…
to die on top…

wanting to blow up…

a hairy cunt shot takes off his shoes…
ending with the throw of a bunny or a ball…
an empty fist mimed with a heavy condom…

the credits roll… his lips pucker… and he is
removing himself slowly from the trojan…

                         (product placement)

putting it up to his mouth… around his lips…
pushing his   cheeks out… his breath…
stretching wet rubber…

how / to / explain / anything / to / anyone / anymore?

a / boy / or / rather / a / young / artist / films / himself / pressing / record / on / a / camera
pressing / record / we / see / the / boy / an / artist / capture / himself / on / a / tripod

walking / away / towards / a / chair / and / a / smiling / bunny / on / a / box
facing / the / bunny / on / the / box / on / the / chair / the / boy / speaks

he / speaks / to / the / bunny / on / the / box / on / the / chair / in / movements / of / the / mouth
he / mouths / with / no / sound / or / rather / the / sound / of / buzzing / hair / heard / elsewhere

and / the / buzzing / loudens
and / his / mouth / rouses
expounding / theories /
of / found / art / soundly

a / dry / erase / board / just / is
the / boy / just / knows / it
he / writes / *fort* / *da*
in / dry / erase
marker

he / erases / it
he / erases / *fort* / *da*
he / writes / it / again / and
he / erases / it / again / and / again
he / writes / to / erase / and / vise / versa

his / young / artist / cock / growing
his / young / artist / cock / showing
his / young / artist / cock / bursting

a / hole / through / his / baby / rib / briefs
a / quart / of / milk / plugged / upside / down

this / boy's / not / a / boy
this / boy / is / a / man / oh / my!
the / bunny / on / the / box / remains

grabbing / his / swollen / cock
marker / in / hand / the / boy
slashes / the / bunny / a / mustache

with / a / dumb / smile
comes / a / dumb / summersault

exhibit z: eros

and setting up a camera / he tucks his penis
he tucks his penis / and pulls back his undies
he pulls back his undies / and shaves his pubis
he shaves his pubis / until it is smooth

and pressing record / he pulls out a sharpie
he pulls out a sharpie / and writes on his pubis
he writes on his pubis / the word of another
the word of another / he writes for his mother

he writes *wow* on his pubis / so that he can read it
and *mom* on the file / so that she might know it
and sends it to her / so that she might read it
for knowing he thinks / is rather important

turning in circles / her flesh on his chair
their word as the earth / now his bird is not there

and shhhh!

"it's not nothing" / is whispered quietly
into the ear / of a deaf boy crying
hysterical / over the book's ending

epilogue

it's hysterical
it's absolutely awful
it's art for the ambitiously illiterate
it's almost arbitrary
it's blasphemous
it's a blast
it's two thumbs straight up your ass
it's perfectly asinine
it's bold
it's boring
it's boring boring
it's bald and sophomoric
it's cinematic
it's steroids for the schizoids
it's intersubjective flesh
it's toilet tissue
it's sincerity inside a trojan horse
it's post-body art
it's unsafe
it's completely forgettable
it's infectious
it's everybody poops on mushrooms
it's beautiful
it's haunting
it's impenetrable
it's an epic love poem
it's complete ivory tower nonsense
it's poison
it's brilliant
it's irony even a hipster can't love
it's the new american gothic
it's a whole generation
it's devoid of any insight
it's tautological
it's scathing
it's pure pretentiousness
it's heart wrenching
it's breathless
it's pure representation
it's pure contamination
it's a puzzle with no corner pieces
it's a book length magic trick
it's obsessed with death
it's post-human with a twist
it's theory on the rocks

it's cyborg meets cyclops
it's fucked up
it's the longest shit joke ever
it's not even funny
it's hilarious
it's offensive
it's warhol on coke
it's meet the faulkners
it's smut for children
it's pathetic
it's haphazard
it's dr. seuss on adderall
it's a new form of ethics
it's dada for dummies
it's dumb
it's something alright
it's successful at times
it's revealing at times
it's reveling
it's reviling
it's relational
it's real elation
it's null
it's word play sure but is it fun?
it's a masterpiece of shit
it's unstoppable
it's a battleground of texts
it's an index of language
it's s=t=u=p=i=d
it's playing with ghosts
it's no good
it's a matter of taste
it's tasteless
it's allegory
it's a throbbing package of condensation
it's trying to be important
it's trying too hard
it's lazy
it's half good
it's not half bad
it's self-destructive
it's pornographic
it's the death of flarf
it's flarf for flarf's sake
it's confused

it's sexy
it's melodrama
it's hypnotic
it's directionless
it's conceptually a wreck
it's going to make you cry
it's going to make you want to write
it's totally queer and campy
it's the most feminist work ever made by a man
it's misogynistic
it's aphoristic
it's totally fucking gay
it's totally fucking hot
it's like waking up to a dead phone
it's a pin prick
it's accurate as hell
it's gluttonous
it's melancholy proper
it's self-indulgent
it's self-promotional
it's cheap
it's obscene
it's joyful

CPSIA information can be obtained at www.ICGtesting.com
Printed in the USA
LVOW10s0740270315

432275LV00003B/34/P